Carol,
I saw this and I immediately thought of you. I just wanted you to know that you are in my thoughts and pr... Take care and God bless!

Love,
Melissa

EDWARD BEAR ESQ.

THE TRUE STORY OF THE ASTONISHING ACHIEVEMENTS OF TEDDY

EDWARD BEAR

━ ESQ. ━

THE TRUE STORY OF THE ASTONISHING ACHIEVEMENTS OF TEDDY

MICHÈLE BROWN

Stewart, Tabori & Chang
New York

First published in Great Britain in 1997 by
PAVILION BOOKS LIMITED
26 Upper Ground, London SE1 9PD

Designed by Bet Ayer
Edited by Jo Fletcher-Watson
Picture research by Sophie Dziwinski

Published in 1997 and distributed in the U.S. by
Stewart, Tabori and Chang,
a division of U.S. Media Holdings, Inc.
575 Broadway, New York, NY 10012

Distributed in Canada by
General Publishing Company Ltd.
30 Lesmill Road, Don Mills, Ontario
Canada M3B 2T6

Library of Congress Catalog Card Number: 96-69925

ISBN 1-55670-542-5

Printed in Hong Kong

2 4 6 8 10 9 7 5 3 1

CONTENTS

PREFACE   10

1. LIFE BEFORE TEDDY   13
Distinguished Ancestors of Edward Bear, Esq.

2. TEDDY'S BEAR   19
Origins of the American Teddy Bear

3. BÄRLE AND FRIENDS   26
Origins of the German Teddy Bear

4. "BUTTON IN EAR"   33
The Phenomenal Success of the German Teddy Bear Industry

5. RULE BEARTANNIA   46
The Unique Contribution of the British Teddy

6. BEAR NECESSITIES   62
Teddy Bear Nonsense and Novelties

7. CELEBRATING TEDDY   68
An Icon for the Twentieth Century

8. THE RISE AND RISE OF EDWARD BEAR   77
The Great Teddy Bear Renaissance

9. ME AND MY BEAR   92
Celebrities and Celebrity Bears

10. OLD GOLD   96
Collecting Bears for Profit and Pleasure

INDEX   106
ACKNOWLEDGMENTS   108

PREFACE

Dear Reader,

I was delighted (and rather flattered!) to be asked to write a short introduction to this little book about my forebears. It traces my own history, and the history of my distinguished teddy bear family, from our sudden rise to fame at the beginning of the century, right up to the present day.

The first genuine *teddy* bears emerged in America and Germany at about the same time that King Edward VII came to the throne of England. This has always struck me as a happy coincidence: King Edward, whose nickname was Teddy, was merry and popular like the bears who shared his name.

The teddy bear family has now spread to every corner of the globe. We speak a universal language which is understood by everyone, everywhere, and we have the gift of creating happiness wherever we go. In return for our unquestioning loyalty and love we are loved and cherished by our owners. Our friendships with them last a lifetime – no one is ever too old or too young to hug their bear. As a result we have created such a fund of goodwill that I feel I can say, without any fear of boasting, that my family has become a major force for good over the last ninety years.

As the popularity of teddy bears has grown, a whole mythology has grown with it. I am sorry to say one or two little inaccuracies have been allowed to creep into the story along the way. Here, at last, is a book which sorts out those tiny errors and which tells, simply and delightfully "The True Story of the Astonishing Achievements of Teddy." I warmly recommend it to you, and to all teddy bear lovers everywhere.

Yours very sincerely,

Edward

EDWARD BEAR, ESQ.

Two carved wooden hat stands, each in the form of a tree with a mother bear reaching for a naughty bear cub. These were extremely popular in 19th-century Germany.

CHAPTER ONE

LIFE BEFORE TEDDY

Distinguished Ancestors of Edward Bear, Esq.

The teddy bear, worldwide symbol of childhood, security, warmth and innocence, has an eternal quality which makes us feel it has been with us for ever. In reality, this cuddly stuffed toy, beloved of children and adults alike, was invented in the earliest years of the twentieth century. Although now such a popular item with collectors, teddy bears are not, strictly speaking, true antiques. They are all less than one hundred years old, more modern than the motor car, the telephone or electric light.

The soft-toy teddy bear may be a comparative youngster, but bears have been an object of fascination since earliest times. There is archaeological evidence that bears were regarded with veneration as far back as forty thousand years ago. This is partly explained by the fact that when bears walk on their hind legs they take on a remarkably human aspect. This resemblance is emphasized further by their faces, which have smallish noses, and their eyes, which look out directly in front, just as they do in human beings.

Where bears roamed wild, they were a powerful part of

A Staffordshire glazed jug depicting a chained bear.

local myth and folklore, usually acknowledging some mystical relationship between man and beast. In different parts of the world they were given names which reflected their closeness to the human beings who both feared and admired them. These names included Fur Man, Black Beast and The Strong One. Bears featured heavily in Native North American culture, where they were viewed as gods or relatives and sometimes given a family name, such as Grandfather, to indicate wisdom.

A 19th-century French clockwork automaton in the form of a captive bear. The realistic, fierce-looking bear contrasts strongly with later, more cuddly teddy bears.

Bears seem to disappear in the winter when they hibernate. This phenomenon, of apparently vanishing and then miraculously reappearing in the springtime, led to many mythical stories in different parts of the world. For example, in Siberia the bears were said to be messengers who brought back messages from the spirit world when they reappeared in the warmer weather. The bear's ability to survive the winter without sustenance was sometimes explained by the myth that it could sustain itself by sucking on its own paws. Another myth was that a bear cub was born as a shapeless form which was literally "licked into shape" by its mother. As late as the eighteenth century, the poet Alexander Pope wrote:

So watchful Bruin forms, with plastic care,
Each growing lump, and brings it to a bear.

The expression "to lick something, or someone, into shape" – to get
it in good working order – has become a part of our everyday language.

For many centuries there was a healthy respect for bears and a
desire to pay tribute to these powerful, furry beasts. Naming some of
the brightest stars in the sky after them is an example. Early
astronomers in India gave the Sanskrit word meaning 'bright'
(*rakhi*) to two of the main constellations of stars. But when the
Ancient Greeks heard this name it sounded to them like their own
word for a bear (*arctos*), so they assumed the name of the constellations was The Bear. The Romans in their turn then looked for a
justification for the names, which in Latin are Ursa Major (The
Great Bear) and Ursa Minor (The Little Bear). The story in Roman
mythology which explains their origin is as follows. Calisto, one of

This ceramic tile panel, by the Pre-Raphaelite artist Sir Edward Burne-Jones, illustrates
how, in the fairy tale *Beauty and the Beast*, the beast was frequently depicted as a bear.

A simple hand-carved Russian wooden toy made in the early 20th century. Similar toys had been made for hundreds of years.

the nymphs of Diana, goddess of the hunt, had two sons by Jupiter, chief of the gods. Juno, Jupiter's jealous wife, changed the boys into bears. Unable to turn them back into children again, Jupiter outwitted Juno by giving his two sons eternal life as bright stars in the heavens.

Bears featured on many medieval coats of arms, including that of the mighty English Earl of Warwick. To this day the county of Warwickshire is symbolized by a bear. The Swiss town of Berne also has a bear on its coat of arms and its name is popularly supposed to come from the German word for a bear. Internationally the bear was the recognized symbol of the powerful Russian Empire.

With so much interest in them it is hardly surprising that, long before the teddy bear arrived on the scene, bears were represented in many different ways and materials, including wood, metal and stone. Native Americans carved them on totem poles, painted them on masks and gave small carved bears to their children. Wooden toys, like the popular bears on wheels, were also found in many north

European countries, where they were carved during the long, dark winter evenings when time lay heavy on people's hands. These bear toys tended to be called by their own national pet names, including the usual English name for a bear – Bruin. A simple model bear, usually called Mishka, was the traditional Russian children's toy.

In Central and Eastern Europe bear images were not reserved for children's toys but were found on a variety of artefacts and furniture. Woodcuts of bears, particularly tame or dancing bears, were popular in Russia. In nineteenth-

The modern Coat of Arms of Warwickshire incorporates the symbol of the medieval Earls of Warwick – the Bear with Ragged Staff.

century Germany it was fashionable to own a carved hat and umbrella stand in the form of a tree, with a bear cub balancing on the top branch and its mother waiting anxiously below.

From about 1880 mechanical toys called automata were extremely popular in England, France and Germany. These came in many guises, usually as different types of doll. Sometimes, however, they took the form of dancing bears, which were still a common sight at that time in fairs and marketplaces. As well as dancing bears there were drinking bears, which poured wine from a flagon into a cup, and smoking bears. It is unlikely that these were ever intended as toys for children. Their clockwork mechanisms were far too delicate and expensive to allow children to play with them. And though some of the animals were made of real fur or fur fabric, they invited admiration rather than uninhibited affection and handling. As well as being far from cuddly to the touch they had realistic faces, often with

Two Meissen models of young bears playing.

tongues and ferocious fangs. They were clearly aimed at adult collectors, who admired them for their fine workmanship and their novelty value. Today they are much valued antiques which fetch high prices in the auction houses.

Bear images featured strongly in literature well before the twentieth century. In *Beauty and the Beast*, Madame le Prince de Beaumont's fairy tale written in 1740, the beast eventually turns back into a handsome prince, emphasizing once again the closeness between bears and human beings. In *The Three Bears*, published by the poet Robert Southey in 1837, the bears live a human style of life but nevertheless they are not the adorable and harmless teddy bears we associate with childhood today. Goldilocks, the little girl who wanders into their cottage by mistake, is far too frightened of them to stay when she wakes up and discovers they have returned home from their walk. As well as the classic fairy tales, there were less well-known stories featuring bears, such as *Adventures of a bear, and a great bear too* by Alfred Elwes, which was published in London in 1857.

Over thousands of years bears had undoubtedly established a secure place in our human culture. Yet as the twentieth century opened the bear's finest hour was still to come.

CHAPTER TWO

TEDDY'S BEAR

Origins of the American Teddy Bear

Over the centuries the bear had established a niche for itself as a fascinating but not particularly friendly figure in folklore. How did it turn its reputation upside down and become the universal symbol of love and childhood? How did the new toy with the friendly image acquire its name? And how did it conquer the world?

Arthuritis, an Early Ideal teddy bear, with a typical triangular face.

A teddy bear is fundamentally different from the image of a real bear because it is in no way threatening. The vulnerable appearance of babies brings out the protective nature of adults and it is the babylike qualities of the teddy bear which distinguish it from the bears that went before. Its face is unrealistically wide, more like the smiling round face of a baby. It has a cute little nose, bright round eyes and a compact, soft body with movable arms and legs which make it easy to cuddle. As with a baby, in comforting it we feel comforted, in loving it, we feel loved in return, but unlike a baby it makes no annoying demands on us. In the eyes of its owner, the teddy bear is dependable, trustworthy and loyal. Being a bear, and not a human-style doll, it is not obviously a "girl's toy." Even the most manly little boys of ninety years ago felt able to be seen with one without loss of face. Teddy's unique appeal knows no boundaries of age, sex or nationality.

Theodore Roosevelt (1858-1919),
President of the United States, 1901-1909

Germany and the United States both claim to have invented the teddy bear, but the truth seems to be that it evolved almost simultaneously on both sides of the Atlantic in 1902-3. Since then it has flourished equally in the Old World and the New.

One reason we tend sometimes to favour the American claim to be first with the teddy bear is because the very earliest German soft

Clifford Berryman's *Washington Post* cartoon of
Teddy Roosevelt's hunting trip, which was published
on November 16, 1902.

fabric bears retained their rather intimidating "real" bear face, whereas the earliest plush bears in the United States were very definitely *teddy* bears. The other reason is the origin of the name, which is, without question, American.

We know for certain that in the closing days of 1902 a Russian immigrant called Morris Michtom, who owned a confectionary and stationery shop in Brooklyn, New York, displayed a plush stuffed toy bear cub in his window and called it "Teddy's Bear." We also know that this bear took its name from the twenty-sixth President of the United States, Theodore "Teddy" Roosevelt.

The story of how this came about is a charming one. On 14 November 1902, President Roosevelt was on a hunting expedition in Smedes County, Mississippi. He was there to conduct some tricky political business about the boundary between Louisiana and Mississippi and the bear hunt had been arranged to afford him a little relaxation. President Roosevelt was a popular man and very aware of his image, which is why he liked to be seen as a rugged hunting, shooting and fishing type.

On that particular day the hunting party had had little success and the President had not bagged a single bear. Anxious to put matters right, some of the hunters chased and stunned a 235-pound black bear and tethered it to a tree to give the President an easy target. But when Roosevelt arrived on the scene he declined to shoot a captive animal and declared stoutly, "Spare the bear!"

This evidence of sporting fair play was speedily relayed to the world by the *Washington Post,* which wrote, "President called after the beast had been lassoed, but he refused to make an unsportsmanlike shot." Accompanying the report was a drawing by political cartoonist Clifford K. Berryman, in which the bear appeared as an enchanting bear cub with round eyes and large ears. The cartoon was given the caption "Drawing the Line in Mississippi" to tie in the President's action with his political purpose for being in the State.

As Russians, Morris Michtom and his wife Rose were already very bear-aware. Inspired by the newspaper story, Rose made a jointed soft fabric bear toy with the cuddly appeal of a small bear cub. Morris put it in the shop window as "Teddy's Bear" alongside a copy of the cartoon. It sold immediately, and the Michtoms quickly found they could sell as many bears as they could make.

The story then goes that Morris Michtom sent a letter, with a sample bear, to the White House, asking permission to call his bear "Teddy's Bear." He claimed to have received a hand-written note back from the President granting permission while modestly protesting that he didn't know that his name would be worth a great deal. Since originals have never been produced of either of these letters it may well be that they were a clever marketing idea dreamed up in retrospect. The bear, now in the Smithsonian Institution in Washington, is said to be the original bear made by the Michtoms for President Roosevelt. However, although his longish muzzle clearly marks him out as an early model, he was most probably made by the Michtoms' company a few years later, in about 1907.

President Roosevelt was not a sentimental man and, as his daughter later revealed, he never liked teddy bears very much. But the

President in the White House found the publicity just as useful as did Mr. and Mrs. Michtom in their tiny Brooklyn shop. As the popularity of "Teddy's Bear" soared, President Teddy Roosevelt adopted it as his political mascot during the 1905 Presidential election campaign. He was undoubtedly helped by the fact that Berryman used the bear in most of his later political cartoons about the President.

Sales of "Teddy's Bear" boomed throughout 1903 and Butler Brothers, one of the United States' largest toy wholesalers, agreed to guarantee the Michtoms' credit with the factory which made the plush fabric. By the end of 1903, the Michtoms had formed

An Ideal Toy Company teddy bear.

the Ideal Novelty and Toy Company (known as the Ideal Toy Company from 1938). This company, whose early motto was "When we do it, we do it right," had factories not only in America but eventually also in Canada, Australia and even Japan. It remained a family business until 1982 and closed completely in 1984. On Morris Michtom's death his newspaper obituaries hailed him as "The Father of the Teddy Bear."

"John Bull and his real Teddy Bear," *Westminster Gazette* cartoon.

For the first year or two, the toy trade referred to all the new-style toys as "jointed plush bears" or sometimes as "Bruins," the traditional English name for a bear. But because of the President's energetic election campaign in 1905, the name Teddy Bear (the *s* was soon dropped) gradually gained ground as a general term for *all* soft bear toys. At the end of 1906 a rival of the Ideal Toy Company, American manufacturer E. I. Horsman, advertised both "Imported Teddy Bears" and "Domestic Teddy Bears" in *Playthings*, the trade magazine for toy companies. A phenomenal craze for teddy bears swept through America and after that there was no question of their being called by any other name.

Many other American toy companies jumped in to take advantage of the growing popularity of stuffed toy bears. They included the Aetna Toy Animal Company, the Bruin Manufacturing Company, the Harman Manufacturing Company, Gund Bears (who still make bears today), and, in the 1920s and 1930s, the Character Toy and Novelty Company and the Knickerbocker Toy Company Inc. Early bears made by these companies are sought-after collectables today.

Over the next fifty years of so, American bears were produced in many variations. Mechanical bears enjoyed periods of popularity. Dressed bears – soldiers, sailors, bellhops – were popular right from the beginning. In the 1930s and '40s in America, as elsewhere, bears were made in modern synthetic fabrics (rayon and nylon) as well as traditional mohair plush made from the wool of Angora goats.

Despite endless variations, the American bear has kept its individuality and identity. Put a classic American bear next to a classic German bear and you will generally observe at least some of the following differences: American bears have broad, flattish, triangular heads, usually with shorter muzzles than the traditional German bears; ears are rounder and lower-set on the "corners" of their triangular-shaped heads; their bodies are slimmer and noticeably longer, with shorter and straighter arms and legs; and their feet are round or oval and not elongated like their European counterparts. Early Ideal bears had rather pointed toes, which, along with their triangular heads, help to make identification easier. The naturalistic hump, so much a feature of the first Steiff bears, is only found in the very earliest American bears. It is quite clear that, whichever came first, the American and German branches of the teddy bear family evolved quite separately.

CHAPTER THREE

BÄRLE AND FRIENDS

Origins of the German Teddy Bear

It is to the Steiff Company that Germany owes its claim to be the original birthplace of the teddy bear.

The company was begun by an extraordinary woman, Margarete Steiff. As a child she had contracted polio and was therefore confined to a wheelchair. Despite this, she was determined to remain independent and use her skills as a needlewoman to earn a living. By dint of hard work she expanded her business and began to employ other people, opening her own small factory at Giengen, in Swabia, in

Margarete Steiff (pictured left) working in her factory at Giengen.

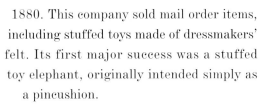

1880. This company sold mail order items, including stuffed toys made of dressmakers' felt. Its first major success was a stuffed toy elephant, originally intended simply as a pincushion.

Margarete Steiff's company grew rapidly and so did its product range. By 1897, the first year the company exhibited independently at the prestigious Leipzig Toy Fair, its catalogue showed stuffed camels, giraffes, sheep, cows, dogs, cats, rabbits, horses and kangaroos, to name but a few. It certainly produced a number of bears at this time, among them a skittle bear and a pull-along polar bear on wheels, both of which were featured in the 1897 catalogue. There were also various

A jointed Steiff teddy bear made in the 1920s.

"dancing" bears standing on their hind legs which were fixed to rotating discs or "roly-poly" platforms. However, none of these early bears had baby faces or cuddly characteristics to qualify as a true teddy bear.

The Steiff Company was a family affair; Margarete Steiff's brother, Fritz, was her main adviser, and all six of Fritz's sons eventually worked for the company. One of these nephews, Richard Steiff, specialized in the design of soft-toy animals, basing many of them on the animals at Stuttgart zoo. At the beginning of this century he designed a toy bear coded Bear 55PB. It was realistic in manner,

Margarete Steiff

with claws and a true bear's sharp-nosed face, but it had several characteristics of the teddy bear for it was made of soft plush and it was "jointed" so that its arms and legs were movable.

A shipment of these bears was sent to New York at the beginning of 1903, only a very short time after the Michtoms had displayed their stuffed plush bear cub. To the disappointment of everyone in the company, the new Steiff bears were initially unsuccessful in America. Paul's view was that they were too large and heavy to appeal to children.

Yet at the Leipzig Toy Fair in March 1903, only a few months later, the Steiff Company achieved a major turning point in its history with this selfsame bear! Ironically the man who brought this about was an American, Hermann Berg, the buyer for George Borgfeldt and Co., a famous New York department store. The story goes that, disappointed to have found nothing special or innovative at Leipzig, and on the point of leaving, he paid a last-minute visit to the Steiff stall. The sample products were already being packed away, but when Berg said he was looking for a new cuddly toy for young children, Richard Steiff searched out the sample of his new bear. Hermann Berg loved it, placed a massive Christmas order for 3,000 bears, and by doing so established a permanent place for himself in the history of the teddy bear.

Sadly there are no existing examples of this very first Steiff jointed bear, not even in Steiff's own museum. Richard Steiff judged the mood of the market and rapidly altered the realistic style to a less authentic but infinitely more appealing babyfaced toy with boot-button eyes, and soft, clawless pads. The new style, which appeared in 1904-5 under the name *Bärle,* was coded 35PB. Very few of these bears or their even rarer small brothers (coded 28PB) exist today, so they are much prized by collectors.

Richard Steiff

By mid-1905, *Bärle* had evolved into an even less naturalistic and more doll-like teddy bear, with a noticeably softer filling. The characteristic curved front paws remained, as did the long feet and narrow ankles. The pads were still made of felt and the eyes were still made of boot buttons. But gradually the hump on the back became less prominent and the long bear muzzle was shortened to give a broader, less threatening face. The new version came in a wider range of sizes, including a large 45-inch bear. It also had the innovative new disc joints. Together with Morris Michtom's bear, Steiff's "new-look" bear established the traditional teddy bear style we all know and love today.

In 1907 alone Steiff made 974,000 bears and the period from 1903-1908 became known as the *Bärenjahre* – the *Bear Years* – in company mythology. Sales began to build in Europe and Britain but America, despite a mini-recession in 1907, was still the biggest customer. By now America had become irrevocably "Teddy Bear Mad."

A typical Steiff bear from the period before 1914.

Inevitably the name Bärle bowed to market forces and from 1908 Steiff bears were marketed as "Teddy" bears like their American counterparts. An amusing little anecdote was concocted in retrospect to give the Steiff account of how the teddy bear came by its name.

Alice Roosevelt, the President's daughter, celebrated her marriage in 1906 with a grand party at the White House. The caterer, anxious to create memorable and attractive table decorations, made a last minute decision to buy up dozens of small Steiff bears. The little bears were then dressed as sportsmen – hunters with rifles and fishermen with fishing rods – as a graceful compliment to the bride's father and his sporting pastimes. During the meal the President was asked what type of bears they were and when he pronounced himself baffled a guest stepped in to explain that they were all "Teddy's Bears." This explanation lends a fairy-tale air to a decision that was really the result of simple commercial expediency.

A "hug" of Steiff bears. Apart from the 1920s bear on the far left, they all date from around 1910.

Some sixty years later the pioneering English bear collector, Peter Bull, visited Alice Roosevelt. This forthright lady stated quite categorically that teddy bears had been totally absent from her wedding festivities. Despite a flat denial by one of the principal characters involved the story persists to this day as part of the fast-growing archive of teddy bear legend.

Whether the story is true or not, we do know that by 1906 Bärle had changed his name to "Teddy" to exploit the craze gripping America. The first stage in the life and times of the teddy bear was complete.

Four mohair teddy bears made in Germany, circa 1910.

CHAPTER FOUR

"BUTTON IN EAR"

The Phenomenal Success of the German Teddy Bear Industry

Steiff was the first European company to make true teddy bears. Since then it has retained its leading position by good organization and dedication. The company patented all their designs, they were scrupulous in ensuring all their products were of first-class quality, and they devised their famous *Button in Ear* trademark which ensured that all their toys were clearly distinguishable from those of their competitors. The words *Knopf im Ohr* (Button in Ear) were patented in 1905 and Steiff has continued to defend its logo and the identifying button with great ferocity.

To combat competition from the many bear-making factories which sprang up all over Germany in the wake of the new teddy craze, Margarete Steiff and her nephew Richard were constantly experimenting with small variations of style and creating new friends for their first teddy bear. The method of making movable joints was improved. The very earliest bears were made mobile by a simple string (or sometimes wire thread) system. Next came a system of metal rods and ultimately, in 1905, disc joints made of heavy card and held in place by metal pins were developed. This solution to the problem of maximum movability and safety was so successful it is still used today.

New fabrics were introduced, and gold plush became a popular option in addition to the original beige, gray or white. Black bears also enjoyed a vogue and were made especially for the English market in 1912-13.

When old teddy bears are dressed in their original clothes this can add
to their character and value.

Individual bears could be commissioned to order. A famous
example is the red bear, *Alfonzo*, made in 1908 for Princess Xenia
Georgievna, the four-year-old daughter of George Mikhailovich, the
Grand Duke of Russia. This bear was sold in 1989 for £12,100
($20,000). It fetched this impressive price not only because it is
unique but because of its romantic history. In 1914 the little
Princess, accompanied by her teddy bear, was visiting her royal relatives in England when war broke out. She never returned to Russia
or saw her adored father again, for he was assassinated after the
Bolshevik revolution. *Alfonzo* remained the Princess's faithful companion and a tangible link with her Imperial family and past until
her death in 1965.

To improve the desirability of their bears still further, Steiff fitted
them with growlers. The early mechanism was a sort of "squeeze-
box" which had to be pressed to create a sound. In 1908 the auto-

Alfonzo, the 1908 red Steiff bear made for Princess Xenia Georgievna of Russia,
seen here without his cossack costume.

matic growler was first used. This worked by tilting the bear back and then forward again. Margarete Steiff even tried to get a patent for a tilt growler which growled the word "teddy," in order to emphasize the Steiff company's claim to be the original inventors of the teddy bear.

Margarete Steiff died in 1909. This was the year that really marked the end of the first stage in the history of the teddy bear – its introduction to the world – because by remarkable coincidence, it was also the year in which Theodore Roosevelt left the Presidency of the United States. After her death, it was left to Margarete Steiff's extensive

A white Steiff dressed teddy bear with black boot-button eyes.

family to protect the company's interests against increasing competition. But despite all their efforts, it was impossible to prevent rivals from making teddy bears. Germany had long been the heart of the toy industry and many German teddy bear companies developed from existing toy factories. Others started up specifically to exploit the new fashion.

Probably the most successful company to prosper alongside Steiff was Gebrüder Hermann (Hermann Brothers), founded after the First World War by Bernard Hermann. The company flourished under Bernard's three sons and remains a successful family business to this day. The Hermann company has always been known for top quality bears and they, too, wished to make their bears clearly distinct from inferior imitations. Because Steiff always acted promptly to prevent other companies using the idea of a trademark button, even if it was not attached to the toy's ear, Hermann used identifying medallions. These have varied in design over the years but since 1952 they have carried the words "Hermann Teddy Original." Hermann bears tend to be slightly "chunkier" than Steiff bears. They often have a clipped muzzle or a muzzle in different fabric from the rest of the bear. Many Hermann bears have the open mouth (sometimes with tongue), which is unusual outside Germany. Two other successful toy firms were also founded by Bernard Hermann's sister and two brothers.

Gebrüder Süssenguth, which was set up in 1894, also manufactured teddy bears with distinctive open mouths. A very early version of their bear, *Peter*, has some claim to being the first teddy bear. Although the oldest existing version of this bear dates from

An early Steiff *Teddy Baby*.
Teddy Baby was designed as a "comical young bear cub with a friendly face." Variations on *Teddy Baby* were made from 1929 until the early 1950s.

1925, a very similar bear is illustrated in one of their early catalogues, well before 1903. Unfortunately *Peter* has a rather frightening appearance, with a realistic open mouth (complete with teeth and fangs set in red gums!), plus a movable tongue and rolling eyes. These features are quite out of sympathy with the appealing friendliness which is so essential for a teddy bear. *Peter* is a bear but, like the nineteenth-century Steiff bears, in the opinion of most experts neither he nor his ancestor who features in the early catalogue would qualify as a true teddy bear.

Other outstanding German teddy bear manufacturers whose bears are much sought after today include Gebrüder Bing, Schreyer and Company (Schuco) and, during the 1950s, the Koch Company and the Anker Company.

Gebrüder Bing started in 1863 as a company making tin kitchenware. From these beginnings it was a short step to making tin toys, many of them with clockwork mechanisms. When teddy bears became all the rage, Bing toys began making their own versions. Steiff prevented them from using a button in the ear as a trademark. An arrow-shaped tag was then used in the ear and this was followed by a stud (Steiff insisted it must not be called a button) in the bear's side, under the arm. The earliest Bing bears have sweet, rather round faces with small ears and short snouts. Later Bing bears have longer, flat-topped snouts and are closer in appearance to Steiff bears.

Because of their established expertise in making mechanical toys Bing made many bears with wind-up clockwork mechanisms. These included acrobats, skaters and a tumbling bear similar to the 1909 Steiff somersaulting bear. The Bing Company went bankrupt in 1932 during the world slump, so their bears are now comparatively rare and highly collectable.

A 1960s Hermann & Co. teddy bear. Although it has the same Y shaped mouth as Gebrüder
Hermann bears, its distinctive triangular chest label confirms its origins. In 1979 the firm
changed its name to Hermann-Spielwaren.

A Schuco *Yes/No Bear* made in the 1950s when this type of bear was renamed *Tricky Bear*. This is a musical example, with a fixed wind-up mechanism visible on the chest.

Schreyer and Company was founded in 1912 by Heinrich Schreyer and Heinrich Müller. In 1921 they registered the trademark "Schuco." Müller had worked for Bing and so Schreyer and Company used this expertise to specialize in mechanical bears.

The outbreak of the First World War in 1914 marked a turning point in teddy bear history by putting a stop to the German domination of the teddy bear scene. German factories were turned over to war work, raw materials were in short supply and export was impossible. Even when the war ended in 1918 shortages meant that bears were made from materials other than traditional high quality mohair. Some were even made of an inferior material called paper-plush.

However, by the mid-1920s German manufacturers were back on course. During the next phase of the teddy bear's history, between the two World Wars, bears were made in a greater variety of styles than ever before. The teddy bear's face became even less realistic as German teddy bears moved closer in appearance to their baby-faced American cousins. German bears of the 1920s and '30s have much sweeter, babylike faces than most pre-war examples. Although all generalizations have their exceptions, when identifying and dating teddy bears, one feature of this generation of bears is that they have glass eyes rather than the black boot buttons of the earlier toys.

The mohair plush used to make the bears at this time tended to be very long and luxuriously silky. Bing in particular liked to make their bears with high quality fabrics. Pastel-coloured mohairs became fashionable, particularly yellow, baby pink and baby blue. A greater variety of materials, including cotton plush, were used. Also dating from this time, and still popular today, is two-toned "tipped" mohair, which gives the fur a delightful textured and natural effect. A famous example is a bear called *Happy Anniversary*, a 1926 Steiff in brown tipped mohair. *Happy* was bought by American collector Paul Volpp in 1989 as a wedding anniversary present for his wife. It cost what was then the highest price ever paid for a bear, $90,000 (£55,000).

Ribbons and bows became a standard adornment to give the bears extra appeal. Dressed bears, which had been popular before 1914, again enjoyed a vogue and bears were produced wearing dresses, sailor suits and soldiers' uniforms. Bing specialized in dressed bears. The idea of dressing bears was taken a step further with many firms producing teddy bear accessories

A rare Gebrüder Bing clockwork bear, dating from around 1910. Note the identifying button just visible on the side seam.

such as bear-sized suitcases, pyjamas, hair brushes, spectacles, parasols and umbrellas. These innovations did a great deal to re-establish German bears in the all-important American market-place.

The most famous Schuco bear, the *Yes/No Bear*, whose tail operated a mechanism to make the head nod or shake from side to side, dates from 1921. The *Yes/No Bear* was a major success for Schuco and reappeared over the years in many variations including a *Yes/No Bellhop Bear* in a smart red and black uniform (1923), which is much sought after by collectors. In the 1950s, *Yes/No Bears* were called "Tricky" bears.

In 1924 Schuco added miniature bears to their range of traditional and mechanical bears. Some of these miniatures were simply tiny conventional bears. Others, which were particularly popular in the 1930s, hid surprises like lipstick cases, powder compacts, perfume bottles and even small pots of jam! In 1936 Germany's political climate led Schreyer and Company to cease trading. It started up

A 1970s synthetic-plush bear made in Germany. It has the open muzzle found mainly on German bears and a "talking" mechanism.

A teddy bear Christmas. Note the teddy bear decorations on the Christmas tree.

again after the war with an American branch importing products from the German factory. Despite initial success, Schuco could not compete against cheaply produced mechanical toys from the Far East and the company finally went bankrupt in 1972. Sadly even the magical world of teddy bears is not entirely immune to the problems and tragedies of the outside world.

German teddy bears, like their American and British counterparts, developed and changed rapidly throughout the 1950s, '60s and '70s. There was a trend away from the pure traditional style. This was partly due to inevitable variations in fashion after half a century of making a very specific product. Steiff, Hermann and other German manufacturers (as well as rival American and British companies) had been forced by wartime restrictions and technological advances to make bears in fabrics such as rayon and sheepskin, as well as natural mohair. The demand for greater hygiene meant that bears were not always filled with traditional kapok or wood-wool but stuffed with foam, polyester or similar machine-washable materials.

Change was also triggered by the competition from cheap, mass-produced bears from the Far East, where there were no qualms about breaking away from the "rules" which governed the appearance and manufacture of a quality, traditional teddy bear. The established style of German bears was strongly influenced by the new style of the rival imported soft toys. All these factors contributed to a more cuddly type of bear in the post-war years.

Steiff began making bears such as *Jackie,* a cub design brought out in 1953 to celebrate the fiftieth anniversary of the teddy bear. *Jackie* had a much rounder face than the classic teddy, the body was short and plump, and the legs were short, with rounder paws than the early bears. In the same year Hermann produced a similar bear, with a short body, arms and legs. *Soft-Bear* was another example of Steiff adapting to the new market; he had a very soft filling and only his arms were movable. In 1957 Steiff brought out *Cosy-Teddy* with a soft synthetic filling, again catering for the soft-toy market. One of the most successful Steiff bears from this period was the *Zotty* (shaggy) bear, which had the traditional German open mouth but the modern style soft body.

Over a period of sixty years, the teddy bear had been refined and developed. It had conquered the world, becoming one of the most recognizable icons of the twentieth century. The German teddy bear

A Steiff *Zotty* bear with two young friends. The *Zotty* style, characterized by a shaggy mohair plush and an open mouth, was introduced in 1951.

industry had adapted to change and survived two world wars, remaining pre-eminent in the creation of high quality authentic teddy bears. Yet during the 1960s it became clear that low-priced, mass-produced bears were not simply affecting the appearance of the new generation of bears, they were beginning to threaten the very survival of the traditional handmade bear.

CHAPTER FIVE

RULE BEARTANNIA

The Unique Contribution of the British Teddy

The love affair between the British and the teddy bear goes back to the first decade of the twentieth century, when the first Steiff bears were imported from Germany. It is not the only country outside the United States and Germany to have made teddy bears; France, Austria, Holland and Australia are just some of the countries that have produced excellent bears. But after America and Germany, Britain has done most to advance the teddy bear's fame and popularity by creating teddy bear characters, like Winnie-the-Pooh and Paddington, which are known and loved throughout the world.

The company which claimed to have made the very first British plush teddy bear was J. K. Farnell. Josef Eisenmann, the sole importer of Steiff bears into Britain, could not get enough German bears to meet the overwhelming demand. He persuaded the son and daughter of J. K. Farnell to change their production over from house-hold goods to toys, and they began making their first teddy bears in 1908.

Other companies quickly followed suit including the British United Toy Manufacturing Company, W. J. Terry (Terryer Toys), and the East London Toy Factory. Unlike the Germans, British firms were not careful about putting labels on their bears when they first began making them. Bears were definitely being made from around 1908 but no British bears of this period can be positively identified and dated, so although J. K. Farnell's claim is widely accepted, it cannot be proved for certain.

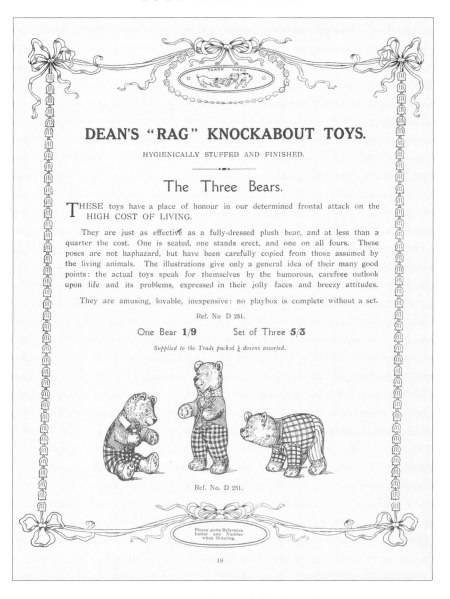

DEAN'S "RAG" KNOCKABOUT TOYS.

HYGIENICALLY STUFFED AND FINISHED.

The Three Bears.

THESE toys have a place of honour in our determined frontal attack on the HIGH COST OF LIVING.

They are just as effective as a fully-dressed plush bear, and at less than a quarter the cost. One is seated, one stands erect, and one on all fours. These poses are not haphazard, but have been carefully copied from those assumed by the living animals. The illustrations give only a general idea of their many good points: the actual toys speak for themselves by the humorous, carefree outlook upon life and its problems, expressed in their jolly faces and breezy attitudes.

They are amusing, lovable, inexpensive: no playbox is complete without a set.

Ref. No D 251.

One Bear **1/9**   Set of Three **5/3**

Supplied to the Trade packed ¼ dozens assorted.

Ref. No. D 251.

Please quote Reference
Letter and Number
when Ordering.

16

Teddy bears advertised in an early Dean's catalogue.

4 7

A delightful "hug" of bears by the firm J. K. Farnell, which flourished from 1908 to 1968.

The company which can provide documentary evidence of its early history more accurately, and which also has a good case for being the first to make a British teddy bear, is the Dean's Company, which continues to flourish from its base in South Wales where it relocated in 1972. The original company was Dean and Son, Publishers, based in London. They devised the novel idea of making indestructible cloth books for children – Dean's Patent Rag Books – and became Dean's Rag Book Company in 1903. The rag books were an immediate success with parents and nannies. As the 1920 catalogue so neatly put it, "To appreciate their numerous advantages, it is only necessary to come into contact with young children who have reached the age when they wear their food and eat their clothes."

Dean's Rag Book Company quickly added a toy range to its rag books. Dean's *Rag Knockabout Doll* and *Toy Sheets* were cut-out dolls, printed onto the same robust fabric. What could have been more obvious than to offer rag book stories about teddy bears and a range of "cut-out-and-sew" teddy bears.

Dean's published a rag book in 1907 entitled *Teddy Bear*, with delightful pictures by Sybil Scott Paley and words by Alice Scott. The story begins:

> Once Dick and Betty pass a shop
> You may be sure they stare
> For staring at them with a smile
> Is Mr Teddy Bear!

In 1908 Dean's placed an advertisement for cut-out-and-sew rag doll teddy bears in the magazine *Home Chat*. "Mamma" bear and her twin children, "Teddy" and "Sissy," (either light or dark brown) were offered for the princely sum of 1/- (5p) and with the assurance that they were "absolutely British." A year later, Samuel Finsburgh and

Company were advertising a similar cut-out bear made from a sheet of flannelette.

A photograph used in Dean's advertisements from 1907 to 1912 shows a little girl wearing a knee-length apron and dangling a small

The front page of Dean's first rag-book story about a Teddy Bear, published in 1907.

plush teddy bear in one hand. Although this is the only photographic evidence, a similar bear appears in a drawing of a collection of Dean's toys used to illustrate an advertisement in 1908. It is tempting to think that the plush bear was made in 1907 in the Dean's workshop as one of a kind specially for the advertising photograph, and later drawn as one of the collection of Dean's toys advertised in 1908. If so, it would certainly be the very first British teddy bear, a whole year older than the ones attributed to J. K. Farnell. This is an exciting thought for teddy bear historians, but probably the mystery of who really made the first

Chiltern *Hugmee* bears were made from 1923 until the firm closed at the end of the 1960s. This one was made in the late 1950s, before *Hugmee* bears were given plastic noses.

British bear will never be solved to everyone's satisfaction.

Dean's swift exploitation of the teddy bear craze, and their progression from teddy bear books via cloth teddy bears to fully jointed plush teddy bears, was probably in part a result of teddy bear importer Josef Eisenmann joining the board of directors in 1905.

Prior to the 1914-18 war Britain still imported most of its teddy bears from Germany. In 1912, when the craze reached its height in Britain, it has been estimated that anything up to two million bears were sold. Eisenmann would have been eager to encourage more home-grown teddies to satisfy an apparently insatiable demand.

It was the devastating effect of the First World War on the German toy industry that left the field clear for the development of the British firms. Before 1914 British textile mills had been exporting high-quality mohair plush for use by the German teddy bear factories. Now the fabric was bought by the established British teddy bear manufacturers and by newcomers such as the Wholesale Toy Company, the British Doll and Novelty Company and Isaacs and Company.

Dean's formed the British Novelty Works' Productions to make a wide range of soft toys, including plush teddy bears. These early Dean's bears were not marketed as Dean's but sold under the Kuddlemee trademark ("Kuddlemee on Toys has the same significance as the Hallmark on Silver," was their bold claim). The 1915 Kuddlemee catalogue has drawings of the first reliably dated British plush teddy bears. *Master Bruno* and *Miss Bruno* were dressed plush bears, available in white or gold and in three sizes. Like all the best bears they had "voices." Also mentioned, but not pictured, was the *British Bear.* The first photograph of this magnificent beast is probably in the picture which appeared in the 1916 Kuddlemee catalogue to advertise Dean's sand toys for seaside holidays; in the background of the beach scene, lolling against a rock, is a very typical British teddy bear with a long, stout body, straight arms and legs and flat feet. Another wartime Dean's bear was called "The Bear of Russia, Germany's Crusher;" a timely reminder that the bear was a traditional symbol of Russia, Britain's ally in the war.

The 1920s and '30s have often been called "The Golden Age of the Teddy Bear," and this was as true in Britain as it was in Germany and the United States. Dean's began producing plush bears under the Dean's name and introduced their classic *A1* bears. J. K. Farnell expanded their successful *Alpha* line. J. K. Farnell's great claim to fame is that the bear purchased in 1921 by Dorothy Milne for her son Christopher Robin, and known to generations of children as Winnie-the-Pooh, was one of their Alpha bears.

Other famous British teddy bear firms were established in this "Golden" period, often by amalgamating with existing small toy firms. Chiltern Toys was started by Leon Rees and a former J. K. Farnell employee, Harry Stone. They developed the business from a toy company started by Rees's father-in-law, Josef Eisenmann, before the First World War. In the 1920s the company was known as H. G. Stone and Company and used the Chiltern trademark. Later the company became Chiltern Toys. *Hugmee* bears, with

Grandpa Bear, made by the Dean's Company, 1937-39. Grandpa's body is made up of his velvet clothes and he has a mohair head and paws.

their broad, floppy heads and short, chunky bodies, proved the most successful Chiltern range and were made for over forty years. Chiltern bears are highly collectable, particularly the novelty bears such as those with wind-up musical boxes in their tummies or the *Wagmee* bears, whose tails are manipulated to make the heads move from side to side.

Chad Valley, a Birmingham based printing company when it began in the early nineteenth century, progressed from printing children's board games and jigsaw puzzles to making toys and teddy bears. Although dating is difficult, they appear to

With his large head, short arms and soft filling, this is a typical British bear of the 1950s. He was made by the Dean's Company.

have begun making bears during the First World War and expanded in the 1920s by amalgamating with a small soft-toy company called Issa. In 1938, Chad Valley received the coveted Royal Warrant from Queen Elizabeth (now the Queen Mother).

Pedigree Toys was created by Lines Brothers in 1937. This firm already made soft toys but the Pedigree label was to specialize in teddy bears. Pedigree bears developed their own distinctive look: their faces were fairly flat, with short snouts and distinctive mouth

A gold mohair-plush, jointed bear made by Chad Valley in 1977.

stitching which curved up on either side to give the bear a smiling expression. The earliest Pedigree bears had black plastic noses; arms and legs were short and straight, the feet were simply round ends to the legs and there were no paws or claws. Pedigree Toys opened a factory in Belfast in 1946 and bears from this period are tagged with the label "Made in Ireland." The company also opened factories in other countries, including New Zealand, Australia and South Africa.

LAUGHING BABY BEAR

A new conception of a " toy " bear cub, natural shape, will stand or sit in a chair. An art silk line in golden brown and biscuit or black and white.

No.	Price.	Approx. Height.
S1064/2 ...	10/8 each ...	12½ in.
S1064/3 ...	14/- each ...	15 in.
S1064/4 ...	18/- each ...	18 in.

All our Toys are made of the finest quality materials obtainable.

One of the bears featured in the 1932 Merrythought catalogue.

The Merrythought Company, which began in 1930, grew out of the textile trade. W. G. Holmes (whose grandson runs the present factory) and G. H. Laxton decided to create a soft-toy company which would use the mohair fabric they manufactured at their mill in Yorkshire. They invited A. C. Janisch of J. K. Farnell and C. J. Rendle of Chad Valley to join the new company and bring their expertise. Space was rented in a former iron foundry in Coalbrookdale (now Ironbridge) in Shropshire. Their designer was a deaf mute called Florence Atwood, who was a friend of Mr. Rendle's daughter. She created all the patterns for the firm's early catalogues and remained their chief designer until her

The Merrythought factory in the 1930s.
The Merrythought wishbone logo, below.

death in 1949. Some of her patterns are still in use today.

Merrythought is an old word for a wishbone, so the company's trademark is a wishbone. This is found on a button in the ear of very early bears, but later bears have a label sewn on one of the feet. Early Merrythought bears include *Bingie,* a cuddly bear cub in tipped brown and white curly plush, the *Magnet Bear* ("the bear which attracts") and a range of art-silk plush bears in sophisticated shades including Eglantine, Azur, Nil, Mimosa,Venus and

REG.
TRADE
MARK

*Made in
England by*

MERRYTHOUGHT

LTD.

COALBROOKDALE
SHROPSHIRE

ALL MERRYTHOUGHT
TOYS BEAR THIS
TICKET.

A group of Merrythought bears. The large bear is *Punkinhead,* made exclusively for the Canadian department store, Eaton's, 1949-56. He is holding the hand of a red Merrythought teddy bear made in about 1930, whose distinctive web-claw stitching can be clearly seen. The two smaller bears in the front are a *Mr. and Mrs. Twisty Cheeky,* made in 1965, which have bendable internal wire frames.

Clematis, all of them chosen from "the 1932 selections of the Paris Dress Designers."

When the Second World War started the Merrythought factory was turned over to war-work. Production was inevitably affected in all the British toy factories, and even when the war ended, the constraints of rationing restricted what could be made. During the war many people knitted bears for their children using wool recycled from old clothes or made teddies from patterns shown in women's magazines. Although they were rarely made in quality mohair plush but out of any spare fabric the owner had available, many collectors like to buy these unique old bears.

As a result of wartime rationing, bears were made of some interesting and unexpected fabrics by established manufacturers as well. Popular options were sheepskin or a form of cheap plush made from wood-pulp and mohair. From the early 1950s rationing was no longer a consideration but hygiene became important to prospective purchasers. Wendy Boston Playsafe Toys was set up in Wales in 1946. As the name implied, the company specialized in safety. In place of the glass eyes, with their potentially dangerous wire shanks, which had become the norm after about 1920, they created special plastic eyes with screw locks.

Throughout the 1920s, '30s and '40s, kapok had been the preferred material for stuffing the bears as it created a softer toy than wood-wool. Kapok did not wash and dry successfully, especially when the bear was made

A Merrythought *Bingie* bear cub from the 1930s.

of traditional mohair. Nor did the early types of synthetic foam stuffing. However a new stuffing of plastic pellets was used by Wendy Boston when they made the first all-synthetic machine-washable bear with plastic eyes in 1954. This highly successful innovation was quickly copied by other toy manufacturers. Throughout the '50s and '60s bears made from nylon fur fabric were popular because they could be machine washed.

Traditional companies like Dean's, Merrythought and Chiltern Bears adapted their styles and made bears in the new wonder fabric Bri-nylon, which came in a variety of bright fabrics as well as the more usual brown and beige. Merrythought included a teddy in its 1958 *Jumpee* range which was described as "a washable cuddly bear, with a specially soft foam stuffing and made of super quality silk plush in assorted pastel colours."

During the 1960s and '70s, not only the appearance but the very survival of traditional British bears, like their counterparts in America and Germany, was threatened by the influx of cheaper soft toys imported from the Far East. Several firms closed down altogether, including J. K. Farnell, which made their last bears in 1968. In 1967 Chiltern Toys was taken over by Chad Valley, which in turn was taken over by Palitoy in 1978; Palitoy was later sold to an American firm. Wendy Boston Playsafe Toys closed in 1976. Pedigree Toys survived for some years in the hands of various different owners, but finally ceased trading completely in 1988.

To combat the competition from abroad those established firms which survived felt pressure to make washability and softness their priorities and to cut corners on the expensive process of making a hand-finished bear. So it is perhaps not totally surprising that the traditional appearance of the teddy bear was threatened during the post-war period. For collectors, most of the imported mass-produced bears do not qualify as true teddies and they have no value in the salerooms (although, of course, they make delightful cuddly toys and give a lot of pleasure to their owners).

By the end of the 1970s only Dean's and Merrythought remained of the early British companies, and the future of the traditional British teddy was very much in the balance.

This 1960s Dean's bear was made from manmade materials and came in a variety of shades and sizes.

CHAPTER SIX

BEAR NECESSITIES

Teddy Bear Nonsense and Novelties

In the early years of the twentieth century, the teddy bear rapidly became an essential item for every self-respecting child and for a surprisingly large number of adults. Equally rapidly, everyday items and giftware in teddy bear guise flooded onto the market. What could not be disguised as a teddy bear was covered with teddy bear decoration. In just a few short years, teddy had made the leap from being a novelty to becoming a necessity. We are inclined to assume that teddy bear novelty items are a phenomenon of late twentieth-century commercialism, but this is far from being the case. Right from the beginning, the popularity of the teddy bear was exploited in a wide range of novelty items and memorabilia.

A jointed mohair teddy bear purse probably made between the wars.

The fact that the first known teddy bear advertisement, in November 1906, was for a teddy bear novelty accessory, not for a toy bear, is the clearest indication that teddy's versatility was immediately recognized. This first advertisement, using the expression "teddy bear" (rather than plain "bear" or "Bruin") was placed by E. J. Horsman, who offered side lamps for

A "hug" of classic Steiff bears from around 1910, together with a Steiff teddy bear tea service.

cars in the form of teddy bears. Horsman did not advertise actual toy teddy bears until December 1906. In addition to teddy bear lamps, teddy bear mascots for car hoods, were also popular in the early years of the twentieth century. In 1913 Steiff devoted a whole page of their catalogue to motor car accessories, many of which had a teddy bear theme, including "bear standing on radiator cap" and "bear climbing up the radiator grille." Although they were determined to protect their commercial interests, Steiff was far from purist in their interpretation of the uses to which teddy bears could be adapted. In addition to all sorts of mechanical bears, musical box bears and bears on wheels, they devised totally new uses for their bears. In 1907 they produced a teddy bear with a lace-up middle which concealed a cylindrical metal hot-water bottle. In 1930, a Steiff bear with a body that could fit over a teapot was introduced. They also made pajama cases and beautiful teddy bear muffs for

A 1908 teddy bear muff.

children. The hot-water bottle containers were not a commercial success and as a result they are now rare and highly sought after. The muffs, on the other hand, were a triumph which were copied by many other firms. Versions are still made today by Steiff themselves and by Merrythought, among others.

Purses were another early novelty item adapted from the bear itself, as opposed to being merely decorated with a teddy bear motif. In the 1980s there was a craze for children's school bags in the form of teddy bears which appeared to be riding on their young owners'

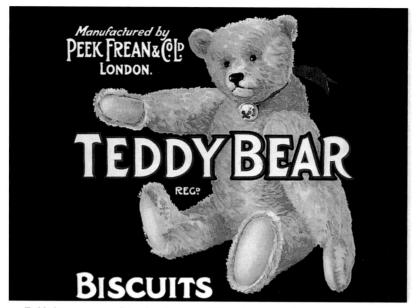

Teddy bears were used to advertise many different products. One company named a biscuit selection *Teddy Bear Biscuits*.

backs. Because teddy bears were perceived essentially as children's toys, the teddy bear theme was applied to almost everything made for the nursery. In America in particular silver spoon and pusher sets for babies were decorated with teddy bear motifs and given as christening presents. Other popular christening presents were teething rings or baby rattles with a silver teddy bear attached. Nursery china sets, decorated with teddy bears, were made by many manufacturers before the First World War and even tinier sets were made for dolls' houses and teddy bear tea parties. Teddy bear money boxes also date back to the first decade of the twentieth century.

For adults, teddy bear jewelry, in expensive gold or silver, or in cheaper costume jewelry versions, was soon available and remains popular today. Jewelry is sold by teddy bear firms like Steiff and

A pre-1914 Christmas card featuring the new toy.

Merrythought as well as by jewelry manufacturers. Teddy bear chess sets have been made from time to time as well as a variety of printed board games featuring teddy bears. Highly collectable are teddy bear thimbles, desk items such as inkwells and cigarette lighters, and dressing table items like hand mirrors.

In the nineteenth century, cheap printing and photographic reproduction techniques were developed. This, combined with the introduction of reliable, cheap postal services in America, Britain and Europe led to the phenomenal growth of the greeting card and postcard industries. These industries took the teddy bear to their hearts and teddy bears became a popular sub-ject. Early postcards and greeting cards are now collectors' items and the teddy bear theme is a particularly popular. Teddy bear playing cards are another greatly prized collectable.

It would be impossible to keep track of every teddy bear related item devised by ingenious manufacturers. Not only did companies make teddy bear products, they exploited bears to advertise any-thing from biscuits to ladies' stockings.

Today the range of bear necessities on offer is more overwhelming than ever, much of it mass-produced. But as well as quantity there is still quality to be had for the discerning bear lover who chooses with care from the new as well as the old.

A jack-in-the-box made by the Dean's Company in the 1990s.

CHAPTER SEVEN

CELEBRATING TEDDY

An Icon for the Twentieth Century

———◆———

Since the teddy bear's debut in 1903 people have been celebrating teddy in music, in song, in literature and, of course, on stage and screen.

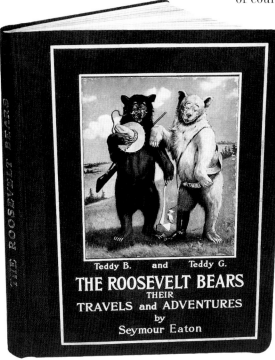

Seymour Eaton's first volume of stories about
Teddy B. and Teddy G.

It was in 1906-7, at the height of the American teddy bear craze, that *The Roosevelt Bears*, written by Seymour Eaton (the *nom de plume* of writer and illustrator Paul Piper) first made their appearance. The books, which began life as a newspaper strip, were verse stories about Teddy G. (gray) and Teddy B. (black), who dressed in suits and looked like American businessmen. They were intended, as

A postcard circa 1910 featuring a teddy bear with two dolls.

Seymour Eaton later wrote, "to teach children that animals, even bears, may have some measure of human feeling."

The role of teddy bears as a force for good is underlined in the story in which the Roosevelt Bears visit England and meet the King. As they leave, the King muses:

> It would help me carry my country's cares
> If every home had Teddy Bears.

Collectors love the Roosevelt Bear collectables such as postcards, which were part of their great commercial success.

A decade later, another American writer, Thornton W. Burgess, wrote a delightful series of books, *The Green Forest Series*, which featured Buster Bear, Mother Bear and their twins, Boxer and Woof-Woof. Like *The Roosevelt Bears,* the stories were full of plain country wisdom, and the illustrations by Harrison Cady show the bears dressed in human clothing.

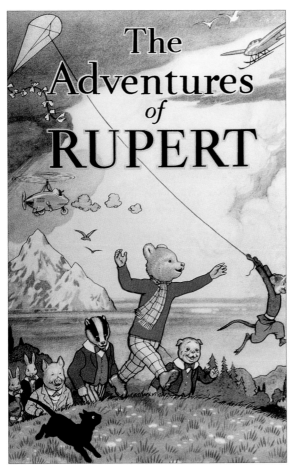

A 1939 *Rupert Bear Annual.*

Newspaper and comic strips were popular in Britain, just as they were in America. As early as 1908, the strip *Bobby and the Woolly Bears* appeared in the magazine *The Butterfly.* The Bruin Boys were created for Arthur Mee's *Children's Encyclopedia* in 1910; they also starred in *The Rainbow* comic when it was launched in 1914 and moved to *Tiger Tim's Weekly* in 1920. Equality among the sexes was finally achieved in 1925 when the magazine *Playbox* featured The Bruin Girls, led by Tiger Tim's sister, Tiger Tilly. Twenty years later, another star bear, Biffo, made his debut in *The Beano.*

But far and away the most popular bear character to appear in a British newspaper strip was Rupert Bear. Half-bear half-boy, he inhabits a magical world where strange and wonderful things are possible. He was invented in 1920, for the *Daily Express,* as a rival to the successful *Daily Mail* strip character, *Teddy Tail*.

Mary Tourtel, who created Rupert, was an impressive woman who, as well as being an artist, was also a pioneer aviator. After Mary Tourtel's retirement in 1935, a number of artists drew Rupert, the most successful of whom was Alfred Bestell, who drew Rupert and wrote the stories for thirty years.

The early *Rupert Annuals* are particularly popular with collectors. In 1996 a mint copy of the *Rupert Annual* of 1935 was

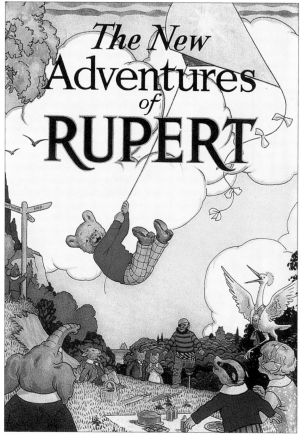

A Rupert Bear book jacket from a facsimile copy of the 1936 *Rupert Bear Annual*.

sold for a record price of £1,610 ($US2,500). Although Rupert is now world famous for his yellow-and-black checked trousers and scarf and his red sweater, the early illustrations showed him in a blue sweater with blue-and-white checked trousers and scarf.

However, Rupert is not merely a curiosity bear from the past; he continues to flourish to this day, having starred in his own television series and videos. He has a fan club called The Followers of Rupert which publishes a magazine called *Nutwood* and Rupert soft toys and gift items are testimony to his enduring popularity.

There is no more famous literary bear than Winnie-the-Pooh, whose exploits have been translated into more than twenty languages, including Latin. Societies of Winnie-the-Pooh enthusiasts are to be found all over the world. The Winnie-the-Pooh books (*Winnie-the-Pooh, The House at Pooh Corner* and *Now We Are Six)* were written in the 1920s by English playwright A. A. Milne, who was inspired by the bear belonging to his son, Christopher Robin. Christopher Robin's mother bought the bear from Harrod's for his first birthday in 1921.

This birthday bear was initially christened Edward Bear. The very first words of *Winnie-the-Pooh* are, rather confusingly, "Here is Edward Bear, coming downstairs now, bump, bump, bump, on the back of his head, behind Christopher Robin." After this introduction he is referred to by his more famous name, and no reason for the sudden change of name is offered to the reader.

In fact, Christopher Robin himself re-named his bear Winnie, after he saw a Canadian bear in London Zoo which was called after its former owner's hometown of Winnipeg, Manitoba. He combined this with Pooh, the word he used for a swan he was taken to feed on a lake near his home.

Even more confusingly the illustrator, Ernest Shepard, did not draw Christopher Robin's Winnie-the-Pooh but used his own son's Steiff bear, Growler, as the model for the drawings. Milne's stories and Shepard's original drawings have become literary classics, although the characters have since been redrawn by the Disney studio. Christopher Robin's very own Winnie-the-Pooh can now be seen at the New York Public Library and Shepard's original

Christopher Robin with Winnie-the-Pooh.

A 1948 *Bobby Bear's Annual*. Bobby Bear was a comic strip character
that first appeared in the *Daily Herald* in 1919.

drawings are on display at the Victoria and Albert Museum in London.

Another English bear, known all over the world, is Paddington, who first appeared in 1958. According to his creator, Michael Bond, he was found on Paddington station, after a long journey from Peru, with a label round his neck saying "Please look after this bear. Thank you." He is very much a bear of his times since his fame rocketed after he appeared on television in short films made using stop-go animation with small models of the bear.

Teddy is celebrated not only in words but also in music. The most successful teddy bear song ever written is "The Teddy Bear's Picnic," which begins with the memorable words "If you go down to the woods today you're sure of a big surprise!" The music was written by an American, John W. Bratton, and was first published in 1907 with the title "The Teddy Bear Two-Step." The tune enjoyed a certain degree of popularity, particularly as a circus theme, but it soared to fame in 1930, when a British songwriter, Jimmy Kennedy, added lyrics to it. The rest, as they say, is teddy bear history.

Countless songs have been written with a teddy bear theme. Among those which have shown lasting qualities are "Me and My Teddy Bear" and the Elvis Presley hit "I Wanna Be Your Teddy Bear." "The Teddy Bear March," "Dance of the Teddy Bears," "Teddy Bear Rag," "Teddy's Coming Home," "There's Nothing Else But Teddy" and "I Wish I Had a Teddy Bear" are just some of the titles which have enjoyed a fleeting moment of fame but are now forgotten. Many of the tunes were written in the first decade of the century when America was caught up in teddy bear fever.

Bears frequently make the leap from the printed page to the television or cinema screen and reach even wider audiences. The first teddy bear animated cartoon was made in 1907 and based on the

An early record of the perennially popular song,
"The Teddy Bears' Picnic"

newspaper strip *Little Johnny and the Teddy Bears* by John Randolph Bray. In 1908 the Thomas A. Edison Company used stop-go animation with real teddy bears to make a short feature film. Walt Disney created his first screen teddy bear in 1924 in a film called *Alice and the Three Bears*. There is now a collection of much-loved teddy bear screen characters, from Paddington to Winnie-the-Pooh himself. Although not strictly a teddy bear, Baloo the Bear made a great impression in the Disney animated film of Kipling's *The Jungle Book*. The Care Bears were created specifically for television and cinema, while the Muppet character Fozzie Bear and cartoon hero Super Ted both began life as television characters.

Nearly a century after the first songs, comic strips, films and books, teddy bears remain enduringly popular as subjects for stories and songs. New characters are created and new stories are published every year. The little bear with the big personality retains its hold on our imaginations, and the celebrating of teddy seems set to continue for many years to come.

CHAPTER EIGHT

THE RISE AND RISE OF EDWARD BEAR

The Great Teddy Bear Renaissance

At the beginning of the 1970s it looked as though the true traditional teddy bear was in danger of extinction. Ironically, its very popularity worked against its survival, as mass production threatened to turn a family of proud individuals with impressive names like Edward Bear, Growler, Theodore, Mr. Bear, Theodosius, Archibald and Lady Elizabeth into mere conveyor-belt cuddly toys.

Yet at the very moment matters seemed at their lowest ebb, as traditional teddy bear manufacturers everywhere were closing down, the seeds of the Great Teddy Bear Revival, also known as the Teddy Bear Renaissance, were being sown.

Earlier generations of children, who had found comfort in the friendship of their teddy bears, were now parents and grandparents. Despite growing older, many of them still felt an affection for their bears, which was intensified by the childhood memories their faithful companions evoked. These "bear-aware"

World War Two evacuees with their teddy bears.

Monty, the World War Two bear. A 1930s British bear, dressed in army uniform, he was carried as a mascot by his owner.

adults were about to become the champions of the beleaguered traditional bear.

Although trends are hard to pin down, many people consider 1969 the year when the tide began to turn. It was in this year that Peter Bull, a larger-than-life British actor with his own collection of much-loved bears, published his landmark teddy bear book, *Bear With Me* (published in the US as *The Teddy Bear Book*). "In a genuine Teddy's face," wrote Peter Bull, "you see at once the loyalty, common sense and, above all, dependability behind it."

The response the book evoked was quite overwhelming and totally unexpected. The author was inundated by letters from adult bear-lovers living in all corners of the globe. In confessing his own passion for teddies he had broken down the taboos which had prevented so many adults from feeling able to admit to a lasting and significant relationship with their own teddy bears.

For the rest of his life Peter Bull was regarded as the ultimate authority on everything concerning teddy bears and was much in demand for television interviews and appearances at important teddy bear occasions. Wherever he went, throughout the world, his 3 ½-

Teddy Girl, a 1904 Steiff once owned by teddy bear pioneer Col. Bob Henderson.

inch-tall miniature Steiff bear, Theodore, accompanied him, riding in his pocket. Theodore was also a regular television performer, like his owner. In 1995 Theodore, with his personal effects, was sold for £14,625 ($23,000).

One occasion when Theodore was not allowed to accompany Peter Bull was when he went for tea with Theodore Roosevelt's daughter, Alice Longworth, to present her with a copy of *Bear With Me*. Mrs. Longworth refused to let any bear in the house, declaring stoutly that she hated them. She confided in Peter Bull, during their talk, that her father had actually been embarassed by his association with teddy bears, although he had been grateful for the publicity it brought to his political campaigns.

Bully Bear, designed by arctophile Peter Bull for The House of Nisbet in 1979.

Shortly after Peter Bull's book was published, he was asked to help design a truly traditional teddy bear in accordance with all the best principles. This bear was manufactured by House of Nisbet (a British firm owned by an American) and named *Bully Bear* as a tribute to him.

A further development in 1969 was the launch of a charity called Good Bears of the World by an American journalist called Jim Ownby. The idea came to him as a direct result of Peter Bull's book, which proved to him that teddy bears were a potent force among adults as well as children and that this force could be harnessed to do good. The charity's aim was simple – to raise money to buy comforting teddy bears for sick children (and adults) throughout the world.

In Britain there was already another rather unlikely teddy bear pioneer. Second World War veteran Colonel Bob Henderson had built up his own bear collection of over 500 bears and bear memorabilia, based around a 1904 Steiff bear called *Teddy Girl*, which had belonged to him and his brother when they were children. *Teddy Girl* (or a miniature teddy bear when the larger bear was not practical) had accompanied Colonel Henderson throughout the Second World War, acting as his good-luck mascot while he fought in North Africa.

Colonel Henderson described the teddy bear as "a silent symbol of love and understanding, so needed in the world today," and he spearheaded what he called Teddy Bear Consciousness when he founded the Teddy Bear Club in 1962. Later he organized the British branch of Good Bears of the World and shared with Peter Bull and Jim Ownby the credit for raising the profile of the teddy bear during the 1970s.

Nigel, a 1930s Dean's bear (right) sitting with the limited edition replica
Nigel, made by Dean's in 1993.

It was during the 1970s that bear-lovers and bear collecting acquired rather fanciful names based on the Greek for bear (*arctos*) and for lover (*philos*). The newly coined words were *arctophile* or *arctophilist* for someone who loves bears and *arctophily* or *arctophilia* for the hobby of collecting bears. Because the words are derived from Ancient Greek, they give the misleading impression that arctophily is a long established pursuit rather than a comparatively new interest.

The custom of holding teddy bear rallies, teddy bear conventions and teddy bear picnics began to evolve during the late 1970s. Many of these early rallies were organized by Good Bears of the World to raise funds. Later the idea was used by a variety of different charities, most without any teddy bear connections, who saw it as an enjoyable way of raising money for their cause while ensuring that their supporters enjoyed a fun occasion.

In 1979, ten years after Peter Bull's book was published, the Marquess of Bath organized a Great Teddy Bear Rally at his stately home, Longleat, in Wiltshire. The rally lasted two days and was proof, if proof were needed by this time, that by the end of the 1970s teddy bears were more popular with both adults and children than ever before in their history.

A "hug"of modern British bears in festive mood.

Delicatessen, the 1907 Ideal bear who starred as *Aloysius* in *Brideshead Revisited*.

Bear watchers also attribute the revived popularity and wider appeal of the teddy bear to the tremendous success on both sides of the Atlantic of the 1981 television adaptation of Evelyn Waugh's novel *Brideshead Revisited*. One of the main characters in the story, Sebastian Flyte, whose family live in a magnificent stately home called Brideshead, has a bear called Aloysius who is his constant companion. Although Sebastian Flyte is an adult he talks to his bear and treats him like a real person. This struck a chord with the millions of people who watched the television serial. The bear used for filming was Delicatessen, one of the bears from Peter Bull's collection. Delicatessen is probably a 1907 Ideal Toy Company bear - a very rare bear indeed. Peter Bull named him Delicatessen because the bear had sat on a shelf in Ladd's Dry Goods Store, Saco, Maine, for over sixty years before being given to him by Mrs. Euphemia Ladd, who had seen Peter Bull and his teddies on a television programme. Delicatessen took to acting with enthusiasm and his director praised him for never being late on the set, never being drunk and never bumping into his co-stars, who included Jeremy Irons, Anthony Andrews and Lord Olivier. So famous did Delicatessen become after all this television exposure that he eventually changed his name by deed poll to Aloysius!

The upsurge of interest in bears was the catalyst for saving the craft of making traditional teddy bears. Appropriately, since America claims to be the teddy bear's birthplace, the revival first began in earnest on that side of the Atlantic. Collectors had begun to search out early bears for their attractive appearance and rarity value. From the early 1980s old teddy bears started to appear in sales in the prestigious international auction houses like Sotheby's and Christie's. This was a sure sign that they were being taken seriously as collectables. But since there was a limited number of such bears available the prices began to rise, putting them out of the reach of many bear-lovers. Collectors wanting similar bears at more affordable prices turned to the established makers, particularly those whose early bears were so sought after.

Serious collectors were not interested in mass-produced soft toys but in bears with the same features and handmade quality which attracted them to the original toys. The result was that new, yet traditionally styled and made teddy bears, were in demand again after a period of decline. The crucial difference this time was that manufacturers were making bears specifically for the adult collectors' market, and not just for children.

In the 1970s and early '80s, before the revival had fully taken off in Britain itself, the British manufacturer Merrythought was creating bears, such as the "*E Bear*," for the American collectors' market. In 1990, with the American market in mind, they launched an International Collectors' Catalogue, which, as well as featuring reproductions of earlier bears, included new traditionally styled bears designed by Jackie Revitt.

In the same year that Merrythought launched its Collectors' Catalogue, Dean's, which was in new ownership, re-organized itself and reflected the new emphasis on old-fashioned bears by reverting to the name Dean's Rag Book Company. Like other long-established firms, they opted out of competing with mass manufacturing and consolidated as a firm specializing in high quality, traditionally made bears. The same path was being followed in the United States by Gund and in Germany by Steiff and Hermann.

The latest generation of bears is now being made with the original features which gave them so much character in the first place. They are of high-quality mohair plush, usually in an authentic bearlike shade. Eighty percent of British bears are now made in various shades of gold, with the brighter "London gold" being most popular, while in the United States traditional beige and brown or, perversely, very bright bears predominate. The new bears are jointed and often have humps like their forebears. Their snouts are more

Eton, a Merrythought Limited Edition of one only, made in aid of the Red Cross.

prominent and many of them growl. Their stuffing is firm and may even be wood-wool as in the very early bears. Atlantic Bears, a new company making bears in Scotland, is an example of a modern firm producing traditionally designed bears. By using wood-wool as stuffing, as in the very earliest bears, they achieve the stiff, upright appearance of the pre-1914 bears which are still the most prized by collectors. Except that very few original bears have survived in perfect condition, it would be hard to tell some of the new collectors' bears from those made nearly one hundred years ago.

There are several different ways in which the collectors' market has been developed and catered to, including new traditionally styled bears, replicas, revivals, anniversary bears and limited editions.

Replica bears, made from existing old patterns kept in company archives, or copied from old bears, are much sought after. This has been a highly successful route for Steiff which has a meticulously maintained archive where all the patterns are kept on file. Each year Steiff makes a limited number of bears from designs which were popular or rare in the past. Examples of Steiff replicas are *Teddy Baby* and *Teddy Rose*, a replica of a 1925 pink plush bear. They also make replicas of individually well-known bears like the rare, red bear, *Alfonzo*. Where patterns do not exist they are reinvented, as House of Nisbet did so successfully with its replica of Delicatessen.

Long established firms create "Anniversary Bears" to celebrate significant milestones in their history, such as Hermann's *Seventy-Fifth Anniversary Bear*, brought out in 1990, the same year in which Merrythought brought out their own *Diamond Jubilee Bear*.

Individual bear artists, usually working from home, design bears which are made entirely by hand, without using even the limited mechanization employed by larger firms. America and Britain have a large number of such bear artists, working as individuals and selling

Modern bears in the classic style, made in Scotland by Atlantic Bears.

most of their work through mail-order or at teddy bear and craft fairs. Among the best known British teddy bear artists are Naomi Laight, June Kendall, Shirley Latimer and Sue Clark. In the United States, where many bear artists flourish, Dee Hockenberry, Sue Foskey and Sue Lain are known for their delightfully individual bears.

Working on a larger scale are the new firms set up to meet the increased demand. These include British manufacturers such as Nonsuch (established in 1979) and Canterbury Bears (established in 1980) and, in the United States, the North American Bear Company (established in the mid-1970s) and Applause, who began making their own bears in 1985.

Both large firms and bear artists create limited editions of specific designs, which, in their turn, become much sought after because of their rarity value. A large firm like Steiff, with a production line, might make a limited edition of several thousand. In contrast, bear artists who make the entire bear themselves soon feel the urge to move on to new challenges, and it is not uncommon for them to make limited editions of as few as five or ten, or even to create one-of-a-kind designs.

An illustration of an early jointed bear, advertised in the Dean's *Kuddlemee* catalogue from 1915.

So great has been the success of the traditional teddy bear revival that countries in the Far East, which mass-produced the cuddly toy versions, are now mass-producing their own traditionally styled bears. Japan, once known only for its fabric-covered, mechanical tin bears, now has its own teddy bear museum in Izu. Among the bears on display is *Teddy Girl*, the star of Colonel Bob Henderson's collection. So after an uncertain period in teddy bear history, the wheel has come full circle, and the teddy bear's influence is stronger than ever. As the century draws to a close, teddy's paw print is firmly stamped on more countries than ever before.

Two limited edition bears by Welsh bear artist, Sue Schoen.

CHAPTER NINE
ME AND MY TEDDY BEAR

Celebrities and Celebrity Bears

Peter Bull with some of his collection of
teddy bears, pictured in a London square.

Mr. Theodore's Teddy Bear Shop

American child
star of the 1930s,
Shirley Temple,
with her teddy.

Amy Johnson, pioneer
British aviatrix, who
twice broke the record
for a solo flight from
England to Cape Town,
holding her teddy
bear mascot.

The Duchess of York (later H.M.The Queen Mother) with a teddy bear
just presented to her for her daughters.

Donald Campbell, who set new world speed records on land and water during the 1950s and '60s, pictured with his engineer, who gave him *Mr. Whoppit* (inset).

CHAPTER TEN

OLD GOLD

Collecting Bears for Profit and Pleasure

Arctophilia, the new word for teddy bear collecting, is beginning to creep into the dictionaries, giving this pleasing, gentle hobby a new air of importance. Unfortunately, a higher profile also means higher prices, as dealers begin to dominate a market which was once a cozy little world of people who loved bears for their own sake, not for the high prices they now fetch in the auction house.

The days of picking up bargains and making exciting discoveries have largely gone. Collecting teddy bears is becoming an increasingly expensive business. Since it is no longer possible to buy an example of every teddy bear design, collectors now have to specialize, as they do in other areas of collecting. For some people nothing will ever compare with the unique appeal of the very earliest bears, made in the pioneering years between 1903 and 1914. But the cost of such bears is now measured in thousands, or even hundreds of thousands of dollars. Colonel Bob Henderson's *Teddy Girl,* a rare 1904 Steiff which was the star

A rare 1920s Dean's bear.

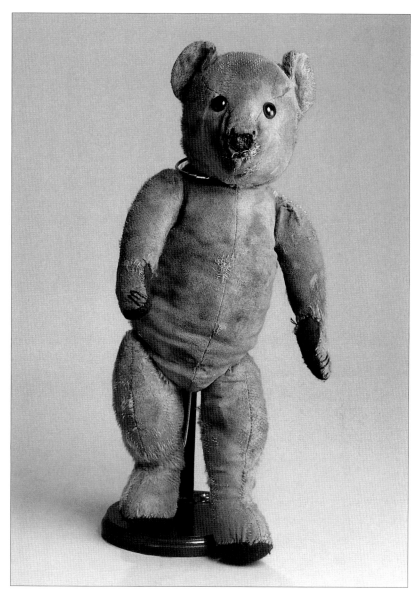

A much-loved British bear dating from between the wars.

Rag doll versions of 'The Three Bears'.

of his considerable collection, sold at auction following his death in 1994 for an amazing £110,000 ($168,000). It was bought by a Japanese collector, Mr. Sekiguchi, for his new teddy bear musesum in Izu. Such prices put the prestigious early bears out of the reach of most bear lovers.

It is more realistic to choose a broader area if you want to build your own collection. Bears from the Golden Age between the wars are also enchanting and there are many more of them, so they are cheaper. Many of the bears referred to in this book, such as Schuco *Yes/No Bears* or Chiltern *Hugmee* bears are examples of prized bears from this period.

A traditionally styled jointed bear, made in mohair and typical of the new Collectors'
Bears made by established firms.

See this widely advertised — highly successful

Dean's 'Childsplay'

BRI*

NYLON

Look for the
TRADE MARK

Regd. TRADE MARK

TEDDY

BEAR

And his many washable
friends all with plastic
LOCK-IN safety eyes.

STAND M 23 THE METROPOLE BRIGHTON TOY FAIR

MERTON TOYS LTD.	CHILDSPLAY LTD.	LETCHWORTH, Herts.
Wholesale Enquiries	Retail Enquiries	Phone Letchworth 4131

The Dean's Bri-Nylon bear, an excellent example of the washable bears being made in the 1950s and '60s.

Some enthusiasts collect miniature bears from all periods; others choose to collect dressed bears, novelty bears – such as purses and muffs – or bears in bright mohairs. If you believe that koalas, pandas and polar bears count as teddy bears, though many enthusiasts insist they are not, you could make your collection of them.

Another possibility is to buy artists' bears, perhaps specializing in one particular artist. Collecting bears by one single manufacturer – especially one which still makes bears today, such as Steiff or Hermann in Germany, Gund in the USA or Dean's or Merrythought in Britain – makes it possible to build a collection from across the range of old and new bears. Alternatively it is possible to collect the quality antiques of the future by specializing in the fine reproductions of classic bears which manufacturers and bear artists have been making since the great teddy bear revival began in the early 1980s. To preserve their value, all new bears should be kept in mint condition, preferably in their boxes.

Mechanical bears make an interesting area of specialization but they, too, can be expensive. Most of the major manufacturers made mechanical bears at some point, from the famous Steiff wind-up *Tumbling Bear* introduced in 1909, to the battery-operated toys made by Pedigree Toys, including their talking Rupert Bear. There are plenty of interesting modern mechanical bears such as *Teddy Ruxpin*, a bear made by the American toy company Mattel, which talks with the help of a cassette. Another American toy manufacturer, Hasbro, has a bear called *Bingo* which talks when it is cuddled.

Japan and Russia, two countries that are not known for quality traditional bears (although Japan did make cheap bears from the 1920s onwards), nevertheless have a reputation for collectable mechanical bears. Constructed from fabric-covered tin, these toys did everything from playing the balalaika to eating ice-cream while walking along or turning the pages of a story book. Their clockwork mechanisms were not particularly strong, so if you make them part of your collection, treat them with extreme care.

A Dean's push-along bear.

As the previous chapters have revealed, Germany, the United States and Britain are the main specialists in teddy bears, but other countries also have teddy bear firms and these could form an interesting area of specialization. The First World War stimulated a small teddy bear industry in Holland and in France, when German bears became unavailable.

French bears from this period tend to have long, thin bodies and large ears perched right on top of their heads. French firms used button trademarks, and names to look out for include PF (Pintel Fils), FADAP (Fabrique Artistique d'Animaux en Peluche) – who both made bears from the 1920s to the 1970s – and Jan Jac, whose best-known bears were made in the 1950s.

Australia now has several interesting bear artists but those wanting to collect early Australian bears should particularly search out Joy Toy Company

A Japanese bear, made in the 1930s, possibly inspired by the Steiff *Teddy Clown*. Japanese bears of this period were of inferior quality and are usually in poor condition today.

bears, which were made from 1920 by a company which was already in business making other types of toys. Not surprisingly, many Australian bears were made from sheepskin. Other Australian companies to look out for, which all ceased trading in the 1970s and '80s when faced with competition from cheap imports, are Emil Toys, Verna Toys and the BerlexCompany.

However you decide to structure your collection, make sure you are as knowledgable as possible by visiting teddy bear collections in specialist museums such as the Teddy Bear Museum in Stratford-upon-Avon, England or the Carrousel Museum in Michigan, America. Museums of dolls or childhood, like the Museum of Childhood in Edinburgh, Scotland, and the Museum of Childhood at Bethnal Green in London, England, are also full of interest.

Your knowledge can also be built up by attending teddy bear auction sales and learning from the catalogue details which have been written by auction experts. You will get an instinct for what bears are worth by noting the prices they fetch at auction. It is also worth visiting the teddy bear fairs which are held in towns and cities all over the world, where you will see a wide variety of bears and have the opportunity to talk to knowledgable makers and collectors. Fairs are an excellent way to meet bear artists and find the latest limited editions as well as stalls selling old bears. Another way to keep up-to-date with new developments is to join the Collectors' Clubs, like those run by Merrythought and Dean's. These clubs produce magazines packed with interesting information as well as making new bears available to members.

There are many excellent books now available which document teddy bear history, how they are made and what they are worth. By reading these you will pick up useful clues to help you identify and date teddy bears you are thinking of buying. You will also learn what makes a bear special. For example, a small number of the pre-1914 Steiff bears were made with a central seam down the middle of the face. This was an economy measure – six bears could be cut from a roll of mohair. The fabric left over was cut to make a seventh but with a seam down the middle of its head. Bears with a central seam fetch more money at auction than their exact counterparts made from one piece of fabric.

Knowing about dating is very important if you are going to be a serious collector. Trademarks and labels are fundamental clues to dating; for example, the very earliest Steiff ear buttons carried a picture of an elephant and not, until 1905, the name Steiff. Materials also give clues; an unusual or inferior fabric such as cotton-rayon is a good indication that a bear was made during the Second World War, when fabrics were rationed. Small details provide useful clues, too – J. K. Farnell, for instance, and later Merrythought used the unusual style of sewing a horizontal line to link up the stitched claws on their bears' pads, but Merrythought bears have only four claws while early J. K. Farnell bears have five claws. When Dean's introduced a growler into their bears it worked by being tipped forwards, not backwards like other firm's bears. Details like these can help you to buy wisely and enable you to identify a really special bear if the opportunity arises.

As well as books there are magazines such as *Teddy Bear Times, Teddy Bear and Friends* and *Teddy Bear Scene* and handbooks, such as *Hugglets UK Teddy Bear Guide,* listing teddy bear shops, museums, manufacturers, bear artists, collectors' clubs–in short, everything of interest to the serious collector.

The most important advice of all for true bear lovers is to buy each bear not for what you think it might be worth, but because it pleases you. Because the expression on its face says "Please Buy Me."

That way, whatever the eventual value of your bear turns out to be in the harsh commercial world, to you it will always be an enchanting friend, and worth every penny you paid for it.

An English hand-knitted bear.

INDEX

*Adventures of a bear,
and a great bear too* 18
Aetna Toy Animal Company 25
Alfonzo 34,35, 88
Alice and the Three Bears 76
Aloysius 84, 85
Alpha range 53
Anker Company 38
Anniversary Bears 88
Applause Company 90
Arthuritis 19
Atlantic Bears 88, 89
Australian teddy bear
companies 102, 103
automata (see mechanical toys)
14, 17

Baloo the Bear 76
Bärle 26,29,32
bear artists 88, 89, 90, 91,
101, 102, 104
Bear With Me 78, 80
Beauty and the Beast 15, 18
bellhop bears 42
Berlex Company 103
Berryman, Clifford K. 21, 22, 23
Bestall, Alfred 71
Biffo the Bear 70
Bing, Gebrüder 38, 40, 41
Bingie 57,59
Bobby Bear 70, 74
Bond, Michael 75
Boston, Wendy 59, 60
Brideshead Revisited 84
British bears, 46–61
British Doll and Novelty
Company, The 52
British United Toy
Manufacturing Company
46
Bruin 17, 24
Bruin Boys, The 70
Bruin Girls, The 70
Bruin Manufacturing
Company, The 25
Bull, Peter 30, 31, 78, 80, 81,
83, 85, 92

Bully Bear 80, 81
Burne-Jones, Sir Edward 15
Butler Brothers 23
"Button in Ear" (see Steiff) 33

Campbell, Donald 95
Canterbury Bears 89
Care Bears 76
Carrousel Museum, Michigan
103
Chad Valley 54, 55, 56, 60
Character Toy and Novelty
Company 25
Cheeky 58
Chiltern Toys 51, 53, 54, 60
Hugmee bears 51, 53, 98
Wagmee bears 54
china 65
collectors' catalogues 86
collectors' clubs 81, 103, 104
Cosy-Teddy 44

dancing bears 17
Dean's Company 47, 49–54,
61, 67, 82, 86, 90, 96,
100, 101, 103, 104
Alpha range 53
British Bear, 52
Grandpa Bear 53
Kuddlemee catalogue 52, 90
Kuddlemee trademark 52
Master Bruno 52
Miss Bruno 52
Nigel 82
Dean's Rag Book Company
49, 50, 86
rag doll teddy bears 49
Rag Knockabout Doll 49
Rag Toy Sheets 49
Delicatessen 84, 85, 88
disc joints 29, 33
dressed bears 25, 34, 36, 41,
43, 53, 58, 78, 100

East London Toy Factory 46
Edward VII 10
Eisenmann, Josef 46, 51, 52, 53

Elwes, Alfred 18
Emil Toys 103
Eton 87

FADAP (Fabrique Artistique
d'Animaux en Peluche) 102
Far East (mass produced bears)
43, 44, 60, 90
Farnell, J. K. 46, 48, 51, 53,
56, 60, 104
Fozzie Bear 76
French teddy bear companies
102

Good Bears of the World 81, 82
Grandpa Bear 53
Green Forest Series, The 69
growlers 34, 36, 104
Gund Bears 25

Happy Anniversary 41
Harman Manufacturing
Company, The 25
Henderson, Colonel Bob 79,
81, 90, 96
Hermann Brothers 36, 37, 39,
44, 86, 100
Seventy-Fifth Anniversary
Bear 88
Horsman, E. I. 24, 62, 63
hot-water bottle containers 64
Hugglets UK Teddy Bear Guide
104
Hugmee bears 51, 53, 98
humps 25, 29, 86

Ideal Toy Company, The 19,
23, 24, 85
Arthuritis 19
Isaacs and Company 52

Jackie 44
Jan Jac 102
jewelry 65
Johnson, Amy 93
Joy Toy Company 102
Jumpee 60

Knickerbocker Toy Company, The 25
Koch Company 38

Leipzig Toy Fair 27, 28
limited editions 82, 88, 90, 103
Little Johnny and the Teddy Bears 76

magazines 24, 103, 104
   Playthings 24
   Teddy Bear and Friends 104
   Teddy Bear Scene 104
   Teddy Bear Times 104
Magnet Bear 57
mass produced bears (see Far East) 43, 44, 60, 90
Master Bruno 52
mechanical bears 25, 40, 42, 64, 101
Merrythought 56-61, 64, 67, 86-88, 99, 100, 103, 104
   Bingie 57, 59
   Cheeky 58
   Diamond Jubilee Bear 88
   'E Bear', The 86
   Eton 87
   Jumpee 60
   Magnet Bear 57
   Punkinhead 58
Michtom, Morris 21-23, 28, 29
Milne, A. A. 72
miniature teddy bears 42, 80, 81, 100
Mishka 17
Miss Bruno 52
money boxes 65
Monty 78
muffs 64, 100
museums 90, 103
   Carrousel Museum, Michigan 103
   Museum of Childhood, Edinburgh 103
   Museum of Childhood, London 103
   Teddy Bear Museum, Izu 90
   Teddy Bear Museum, Stratford-upon-Avon 103
musical boxes 54, 64

Native American mythology 14

Nigel 82
Nisbet, House of 80, 88
   Bully Bear 80, 81
Nonsuch 89
North American Bear Company 89
novelties 62

Paddington Bear 46, 75, 76
Palitoy 60
Pedigree Toys 54, 56, 60, 101
Peter 37, 38
PF (Pintel Fils) 102
Playthings 24
Pope, Alexander 14
postcards and cards 66, 67, 69
Punkinhead 58
purses 62, 100

Queen Elizabeth, the Queen Mother 54, 94

rag doll teddy bears (see also Dean's) 49, 98
replica bears 88
Revitt, Jackie 86
Roosevelt, Alice 30, 32, 80
Roosevelt Bears, The 68, 69
Roosevelt, Theodore 20–23, 36, 80
Rupert Bear 70–72, 101

Schreyer and Company (see Schuco)
Schuco 38, 40, 42, 43, 98
   miniature bears 42
   Yes/No Bear 40, 42, 98
Shepard, Ernest 72, 75
Soft-Bear 44
songs 75, 76
Steiff Company 26, 27, 28, 36
   Alfonzo 34, 35, 88
   'Button in Ear' trademark 33
   Cosy-Teddy 44
   Happy Anniversary 41
   Jackie 44
   Soft-Bear 44
   Teddy Baby 5, 37, 88
   Teddy Clown 102
   Teddy Girl 79, 81, 90, 96
   Teddy Rose 88
   Zotty 44, 45

Steiff, Margarete 26–28, 33, 36
Steiff, Richard 27–29, 33
Super Ted 76
Süssenguth, Gebrüder 37

Teddy Baby 5, 37, 88
Teddy Bear and Friends 104
Teddy Bear Museum, Izu 90
Teddy Bear Museum, Stratford-upon-Avon 103
teddy bear rallies 82, 83
Teddy Bear Scene 104
Teddy Bear Times 104
Teddy Bears' Picnic, The 76
Teddy Clown 102
Teddy Girl 79, 81, 90, 96
Teddy Rose 88
Teddy Tail 71
Teddy's Bear 19, 21–23, 30
Temple, Shirley 93
Terryer Toys 46
Theodore (see also Bull, Peter) 80, 92
Three Bears, The 18, 98
Tourtel, Mary 71
Tumbling Bear 38, 101

umbrella stands 12, 17

Verna Toys 103
Volpp, Paul 41

Wagmee bears 54
Washington Post 21, 22
Wholesale Toy Company, The 52
Whoppit, Mr. 95
Winnie-the-Pooh 46, 53, 72, 73
wooden carved bears 16, 17

Yes/No Bear 40, 42, 98

Zotty 44, 45

ACKNOWLEDGEMENTS

The Publishers would like to thank all those who supplied photographs for this book, particularly Michèle Brown, Merrythought Limited, Dean's Company, V&A Picture Library and Christie's Images.

The author would also particularly like to thank Oliver Holmes, Jackie Revitt and John Parkes of Merrythought Limited and Neil Miller of the Dean's Company for their help. Thanks also to Silvia Coote and all the staff at the Teddy Bear Museum at Stratford-upon-Avon and thank you to editor Sophie Dziwinski and designer Bet Ayer for all their hard work on this book.